The Nasty Woman's Guide to Surviving Trump

NAST T. GIRL

Nas T. Girl
The Nasty Woman's Guide to Surviving Trump

Published by: Nasty Woman's Guides
a division of Bon Mot Books

Cover and Book Design by: Bluesy

Special thanks to Ryan McGuire at
www.laughandpee.com for the fun, funny photos

A CIP record for this book is available from the Library of Congress Cataloging-in-Publication Data

ISBN-13: 978-0-9985530-0-9

For all you nasty girls and women,

and those that support them;

and for Michael Moore and his call to join the army of sarcasm,

I'm with you

She is a nasty woman!

Shut up!

Grab her by the pussy

Sit down, you're fake news!

I'm so fabulous, everybody loves me

I'm gonna build a wall

Mexico's gonna pay for it

I'm not in love with Putin

I've never even been to Russia

Okay, so maybe I slept with a few Russians

They were consenting adults, mostly

"You know, I'm automatically attracted to beautiful — I just start kissing them. It's like a magnet. Just kiss. I don't even wait. And when you're a star, they let you do it. You can do anything….Grab them by the pussy. You can do anything."

—The Orange Menace

1

IT'S THE END OF THE WORLD AS WE KNOW IT (AND WE DON'T FEEL FINE)

Time to put on your big girl and big boy pants (or your stretchy pants if you're an emotional over-eater) and buckle in for a bumpy ride, as The Donald AKA The Orange Menace AKA Putin's Poodle AKA PeeOTUS doesn't appear to be going anywhere soon, despite creating more havoc and hatred in office than any other seated President in history, causing prescriptions of anti-anxiety meds like Xanax and Prozac to go flying off the shelves faster than snow shovels and salt in a Nor'Easter.

In a few short months, Dolt 45 has done everything he can to tank the environment, dismantle health care and fuck up foreign relations. While crying about how unfair he's being treated, Cheeto-in-Chief, who claims he is "like a smart person" despite daily botching the English language, touting fake countries, and leaving high school history teachers everywhere shaking their heads in horror, has managed to break the First Amendment, blab national secrets, skewer science, side with skin-heads, piss off foreign dignitaries, threaten healthcare, ban dreamers and incite investigation for election fraud involving a scandal between him, the Russians and a cast of characters that seem more at home in a David Lynch film than CNN.

The Sunburnt Stalin has insulted every minority and ethnic group imaginable, parading his sexism, homophobia and egoism to the point where even his own cabinet members are shaking their heads and falling short with ways to defend his actions; with the exception of loyalist Jeffrey Lord, who Anderson Cooper dressed down on national TV by saying "If he (Trump) took a dump on his desk you would defend it" – to which Lord just laughed (perhaps he is hoping for a cabinet position, there's bound to be some open spot in the next sixty seconds.)

Nobody, of course, is surprised by any of this. This is, after all, the same "pussy-grabbing" misogynist who harassed and hate-tweeted teenagers while running for office.

However, more people than ever are wondering what to do and how to manage their stress, now that Trumpaloompa is getting into pissing matches with countries that control nuclear weapons.

Stick their head in a drain pipe?

If you're anxious, stressed and worried, like most of America, and would sooner wrap yourself in fireworks and light up, than endure four years with Fuckface von Clownstick at the helm; here's a little levity to lighten your load. A salve, if you will, for that angry hemorrhoid. A handy dandy vomit bag to throw up in – well maybe not that.

Please don't try hurling on this book – save it for your Uber. Puking, no matter how sickened you are at the current political situation, won't make you feel any better, and it may force you to throw this puppy out before you've gotten the great value awaiting you from clean, vomit-free pages and moody back-lighting.

We've got lots of glittery, sparkly, fantasmic ideas to keep every sort busy, productive, or at least pre-occupied for a few precious moments of sanity. Isn't that worth something in these trying times?

And when we say "we," we mean me, of course – I, one seriously pissed-off nasty woman ducking behind this pseudonym because I don't trust that the Tangerine Turtle won't try to lock me up in Guantanamo Bay for using my God given, constitutional, right of speaking out and making fun of him (I worry for you Alec Baldwin).

THIS IS NOT A PICTURE OF ME, IN CASE YOU WERE WONDERING. I HAVE AN AVERSION TO FACIAL HAIR AND I NEVER WEAR STRIPES. BUT YOU CAN IMAGINE THIS IS ME, IF IT MAKES YOU FEEL BETTER.

That's right, it is I, your fellow patriot, who thinks America was pretty great to start with before Golden Showerboy came along.

Has anyone stopped to wonder what this America from halcyon days actually was like that made it that much greater? Are we talking better tasting ice cream? Fast food burgers sans pink slime, or something else entirely?

Are we "making America great again," like back when homosexuality was a crime in most states?

Or back when women were dying by the thousands in backyard abortions before Roe v. Wade?

Or was it during WWII, when we had Japanese Internment camps? Maybe that's the model for the famous wall we keep hearing the Orange Overlord wants to build.

Or maybe Trumperstink is talking about making America like it was back during the Industrial Revolution, when slavery was legal?

While we're at it, at this point, is there anyone out there that Minute Maid Mao hasn't offended?

*ORANGE FOOLIUS CAN USE WHAT'S LEFT OF
THE BERLIN WALL FOR HIS PET PROJECT.*

But we digress (I could really get used to this royal "we" thing – it seems the perfect excuse to shift the blame to someone else, even if you're like an only child and you broke one of your mother's valuable collector's Looney Tunes jelly jars; or if you ate the last Sprinkles red velvet cupcake that your roommate was saving for her ungrateful, conniving, sack-of-shit boyfriend – "we" have no idea where it went; or you end up alone in a room with a bloody knife and a dead body – "we" have no idea how that happened, maybe he fell while running with it or something. You know you shouldn't run with scissors or hunting knives).

Let's get on with this. What's it all about?

2

WHAT'S THIS ALL ABOUT

So, as I was saying, we have solutions for how to survive from now until possibly the end of days (with Trumpaloompa in charge, you never can tell, he threatens to bomb countries that don't even exist; either that or his God complex encourages him to rename countries and battles l'est we all are doomed to forget the Battle of Bowling Green and high tail it to Nambia to get rich and seek health care that doesn't mind pre-existing conditions.)

These are real, tangible things you can do – and we're not just talking about spending the next four years barricaded inside your bedroom with enough Nutella, booze and refined sugar to keep you busy until it's over (although, that is actually a strategy for those who happen to have

Agoraphobia and are not prone to alcoholism or diabetes – you'd be surprised how many times those worlds collide. Seriously. Put down the 20 year-old Twinkie, it gets better... just hold out a few more years).

In addition to words, we have pictures.

I AM FIERY CHEETOHEAD, HERE ME ROAR.

Not a ton of pictures. Not like an art gallery worth – this isn't the Met, or MOMA, or the Broad. And we're not talking about Melania's nude photo spread.

And no, this is not a picture book or a graphic novel, despite you possibly finding it in that category on Amazon – in which case, it definitely, most certainly is a graphic novel with pictures in it.

This book is just about answers, plain and simple. Solutions to your Pumpkin Spice President problem. And when he starts redecorating the Oval in red chintz and gold lamé you'll be needing something to get you through the night, and the day.

Disclaimer, we were going to call this book *"101 Ways to Survive the Trump Presidency,"* but we couldn't think of that many and *"A Bunch of Ways to Survive Trump's Presidency"* or *"A Butt-load of Ways to Survive Trump"* didn't have quite the same ring. Besides, *"we"* are a Nasty Woman, most definitely – and proud of it.

Another disclaimer, if you follow any of these methods and you in fact don't survive Hair Gropenfuhrer's presidency, we are not responsible. We didn't vote for him. It's not our fault. We voted for Hillary. Like the real President, Barrack Obama, we too wouldn't have trusted a man who can't handle a Twitter account with the nuclear codes. God Bless America. God Bless us all, everyone.

One very last disclaimer (we promise), if you do follow one of these carefully thought out methods and end up surviving Trump's presidency as a result, can you please like us on Yelp? We can be found listed under *"End of the World Solutions and Survival Guides."*

3

WHY IS THIS BOOK DIFFERENT THAN ALL OTHER BOOKS?

Why is this book different than all other books? Because with all other books, you might be able to read in a library, or on a bus, or at a snarky dentist's office, but this book, you can read anywhere. You can read it sitting, or reclining; standing, or using your new Shark-supported, sphincter-unkinking squatty potty.

Because with all other books you might have to watch what you eat while reading, but with this book, you can read while noshing on anything you want – bagels, pizza, pancakes, waffles, egg salad, Korean BBQ, a rack of ribs, Portobello mushrooms, gelato, spumoni, red bean paste mochi, a jelly doughnut, a baby bundt, cake, figs, clam chowder, butternut squash, a pineapple, gum, uni with quail egg, a bologna sandwich, raisin pie.

It's entirely up to you -- you have no restrictions on what to eat while reading this book whatsoever, unless you are diabetic or have a heart condition or high cholesterol, and then you still have to listen to your doctor. I mean, we don't have a medical degree or anything like that so what are you listening to us for? Go vegan. Save yourself.

Because all other books may be ones that you might not want to get what, but this one, you can read in the rain with an umbrella. Or covered in the brine of your own rancid sweat while barreling down a road to nowhere on a treadmill at the gym.

Or you can read it while dipping it in the vast saline saltmarsh of your own tears when you think about how screwed we all are going to be since Trumpernickus cancelled all plans to stave off global warming and now the weather's all screwed up and half the country's doomed to fall into the ocean in the next big quake or tsunami or hurricane. It's okay to cry while reading this book, in fact, it's encouraged.

You can even read this book at a Baby-hands rally (though we suggest taking precautions, like maybe wearing a bullet-proof vest, having an armed guard accompany you or be covered in camouflage, so as not to encourage the ire of ignorant lobotomized drones surrounding you. Think of what you'd wear to a Walking Dead party and you're on the right track).

And while we're at it, you should know—

You can read this book on a plane, in the rain, with glasses, of course, or even on a horse.

You can read this book here or there. You can read this book everywhere.

You can read this book while watching CSPAN.

It might give you solace – if you have no plan. Or think it's all a sham. Or like to eat SPAM or ham. Or miss George Michael of Wham!

You will like reading this book, so we say. You will like it because it is different – okay? (Oy Vey!)

4

WHO IS THIS BOOK FOR ANYWAY?

Do you find yourself panicked, depressed, angry, exhausted, demoralized and defeated more and more each day since Trump took office?

Then read this book.

Are you sick of staring at your stack of "I'm with Her" buttons? Find yourself mournful every time you look at your "Nasty Woman" t-shirts and pussy hats?

Again, read this book.

Are your friends on Facebook shaming you for not being more active and joining protest walks, despite being shown evidence that your marching shoes have holes in them?

Perhaps you're seething and sulking but your thyroid is underactive; or you've drank so many energy drinks and artificial sweeteners that your broken-down metabolism forces you to eke out an existence akin to a slug with a hangover.

Read this book between naps.

Maybe you have the social media prowess of a Baby Boomer.

It's not your fault, go watch a DVD or video tape, Jazzercise, then read this book.

Do you find yourself powerless, wondering if the world will be nuked by the Dotard tomorrow?

Read the book.

If you are from another country but now are nervous because Don the Con is hellbent on scapegoating anyone and everyone; trying desperately to incite hatred and xenophobia in the masses as a way of deflecting the fact that he has no idea what he is doing and how he will deliver on the false promises he has made –

Read this book and share with your many concerned neighbors. Translate if necessary.

If you're LGBTQ, Muslim, Jewish, Black, Mexican, overweight, disabled, a woman, or any part of any one of the myriad groups of people Orangina has targeted, attacked, or disparaged –

Read this book. You are not alone.

If you are a U.S. citizen who didn't vote for Trump but can't understand why everyone's complaining and feel like maybe if we just give him a chance everything will be fine – put this book on a shelf for later when you'll need it. And you will need it. Soon.

If you actually like Trump and think he is doing a great job as President – Return this book.

Seriously. You're hopeless.

For everyone else out there who is having trouble coping, or even finding it a challenge getting out of bed in the morning, here are a set of tangible solutions (not 100 of them, but close enough) that will help you get through the night, if not the duration of Trump's reign. Cheer up, there's always the promise of impeachment to live for.

In the meantime, "Don't suffer in silence, heed one of the many methods of survival. It may not exactly be what you want—

"But if you try, sometimes, you just might find you get what you need. Yeah, Baby."

—*MICK JAGGER AND KEITH RICHARDS, TWO*
BRITISH DUDES WHO KNOW A LOT ABOUT
SURVIVING... AND ROCK AND ROLL.

5

SOLUTIONS TO SURVIVING THE TRUMP PRESIDENCY

(SOMETHING FOR EVERYONE)

Since there's no one, fool-proof method to surviving this fool, we've broken it down into personality type, personality disorder, temperament, temperature and pain tolerance.

So, without further ado, here are our survival solutions – in no particular order.

For Those in Denial

Surround yourself with Hillary shirts, bumper stickers, posters. Block out all traditional and social media. Get rid of your newspaper subscription, magazine subscriptions, TV set, radio, tablet, iPhone. Keep only a computer that has no internet connection and maybe an old Gameboy hand-held set for amusement.

Lock yourself in a cabin in the back woods of northern New Hampshire, preferably on a rural route where the mailman won't even dare to show up and where the nearest neighbor is a dental-challenged, anti-social native, a good half mile away and his place is staked out with barbed wire and "Trespassers Will Be Shot" signs.

For the Dog Lover

Get a dog.

Not just any dog, a rescue dog.

Get the neediest rescue dog you can, save it from death row and then spend every ounce of your attention and money on taking care of the dog and providing it with the best life you can think of.

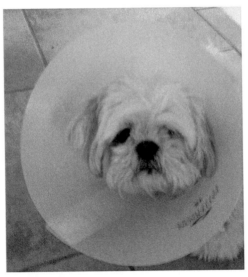

Spend all of your time with that dog. Create special playdates and parties for it where there are baked goods for dogs (in fact, bake them yourself using only organic ingredients).

Take your dog on trips and vacations. Take lots of pictures.

Make your dog his own website and give him a Facebook page and Instagram account, where you will only discuss him and his life.

Or maybe raise rabbits.

For the Hobbyist

Take up gardening to grow your own food and get a few chickens for fresh eggs, to limit your trips to the store, where there will be newspapers blaring disturbing headlines.

Learn to crochet or knit to pass the time. Maybe get yourself some sheep so you won't have to go to the store for wool, besides taking care of your new flock will give you something else to think about than how the country is going down the toilet.

IT'S A PET, IT'S A SWEATER, IT'S A PET AND A SWEATER.

While you're at it, craft some Mexican worry dolls (the people of Mexico have been on this full time ever since the Fanta Fascist took office).

For Singles Ready to Mingle

Rumpus's America is ripe for those looking to pair up. Where-as B.T. (Before Trumpus), you would get stuck on those blind dates where things were awkward and you didn't know if you were right for each other, now there's an instant opening into the soul. A boat straight to the heart of darkness or a window into psyche.

Start talking politics immediately and you will know if you need to bail. No need for the fake phone call, or training your cat to fake-butt dial you as she's hocking up her last hair ball. If your date starts in on how climate control is really a hoax, or bitches about the traffic caused by an anti-Trump rally, or aggrandizes on the wisdom of the Donald's latest twat tweet, just get up and go, no questions asked. Look at all the time you save.

*WE DON'T ADVOCATE VIOLENCE. EVEN WHEN
YOU FEEL LIKE MAKING STUPID GIFS FOR TWITTER OF
YOU PUNCHING BABYHANDS IN THE FACE, DON'T. IT'S
CHILDISH AND BENEATH YOU, AND HE'LL PROBABLY SICK
HOMELAND SECURITY ON YOU FOR HURTING HIS FRAGILE
EGO. BESIDES, THE FOLKS AT CNN GET FIRST DIBS.*

Also, on the flip side, the collective chaos
gives you something to instantly bond over. No
more funky segues and boring small talk, you
can right away agree that things are insane and
the world's going to hell in a handbasket.

That's another thing, what if our days of doom
really are numbered, now that Agent Orange

has the keys to the nuclear codes? Do you really want to be alone and celibate during the end of days? Of course you don't. And why should you? Between all the dating apps and TV bachelor and bachelorette match-ups going on, there's enough people out there to pair up so amp up that social calendar of yours and get to it.

For the Stand-up Comedian

Create a one man or one woman show espousing all of your angst, worry and anger and transform it into humor and satire. Just be careful you don't piss off President Urine-Town with any images too shocking lest you lose all of your sponsorships, funding and any future job prospects in this century because freedom of speech is only applicable if it's not "crossing the line" of what SCROTUS could consider "poor taste.

Remember, this is the guy that makes fun of people's physical handicaps for sport and brags about grabbing women by the pussy all in good fun locker room banter – and can get a good laugh at anyone being made fun of but himself. Proceed with caution.

Best to have a backup career plan and some money socked away when it's time to escape to that nice little foreign island somewhere when the shit hits the fan (if there are any left that global warming's hurricanes haven't decimated by now).

Don't depend on "freedom of speech" to save you. That only works if you're the one in charge; we're talking to you Kathy Griffin. We miss you on those squatty potty commercials, Girl.

For the Twitter Obsessed

Follow @RealDonaldTrump and tell him what you really think. Answer every inane message with Tweets of logic. Run him down with rhetoric. Tweet, Tweet and Tweet again. Resist!

For the Old School Soul

Start reading the classics – Orwell's 1984 is a must, as are the works of Steinbeck and Sinclair Lewis.

Facebook and Twitter will just get you out of

your groove; and all that fake news and alt news and newsy news is bound to flatten your funk.

For pure escapism – well, escape. Turn off technology and tune out. Listen to your old CDs, or watch DVDs for pleasure. Think of the money you will save on cable. You'll need that for healthcare now that Trumpaloompa is going to screw you on that.

Work from home as an artist, or writer, or editor, or nature photographer, or fur trapper, or animal trainer, or horticulturist, or ice fisherman, or entomologist, or Sanskrit book translator.

If you work on the computer (that has no internet), mail in your work and collect your checks from a PO Box that you need to drive

30 minutes to get to, while you pick up monthly supplies.

Live in your own Shangri-La. Pretend Squirrelwig never happened and maximize your state of bliss with some purposeful ignorance.

STOP WAXING AND GROW OUT YOUR FACIAL HAIR.

If anyone wanders on your doorstep trying to mess with your inner peace, threaten to shoot them. (Keep a registered rifle at the door — also handy if you get snowed in and have to shoot a bear or wild animal in order to avoid having to gnaw on your own leg to keep you from starving to death.)

The world is what you make of it. Live free or die hard.

For the Disney Fan

Take a 4-year long Disney cruise to far away, exotic locations — though there's no need to ever get off the ship and leave the magical floating kingdom.

Watch only Disney films and sing along with Disney songs on a daily basis. Imagine yourself as your very own Disney character and make "A dream is a wish your heart makes" your mantra, along with "Hakuna Matata."

Wear adult-size costumes of Disney Princesses or Star Wars licensed merchandise only (if so, make sure you carry a light saber with you wherever you go).

Start every morning by singing "Let it Go" at the top of your lungs before launching into a day full of Pluto's Pilates, buffet dining and Mad Hatter tea parties.

WE REALIZE THIS LEMUR HAS NOTHING TO DO WITH A DISNEY MOVIE. ON THE OTHER HAND HE IS CUTE, PLUS THIS WAY WE WON'T GET SUED. BESIDES, DIDN'T YOU EVER SEE ZABOOMAFOO?

If you have any concerns about going the

distance, have no fear – falling asleep every night being lulled by the ocean waves and the distant refrain from *It's a Small World* will numb you into submission enough to exist in a Mickey Mouse shaped world.

For the Netflix Nut

Convince yourself that this was all just an episode of the new "Black Mirror, San Junipero Pt. 2, San Onofre" where we are all living in the aftermath of a nuclear explosion off the California coastline and are actually dead, but we don't know it yet. How else can we explain Yam Vadar as our leader?

Never mind that Amazon has moved *The Man in the High Castle* over to the documentaries section – this is Netflix! There's plenty here to keep your mind numb to what's going on outside. Comedies, foreign films, original series -- watch every episode of *Friends,* twice.

In fact, maybe you should just lock yourself in a room with an active Netflix account and binge watch everything they have for the next four years – except for *House of Cards,* that might be hitting it a little too close to home.

For the Insane

Lobotomize yourself with instructions you find off the internet. All you need is a sharp tool, like an ice pick or a pointed screw driver, and a good, sturdy mallet.

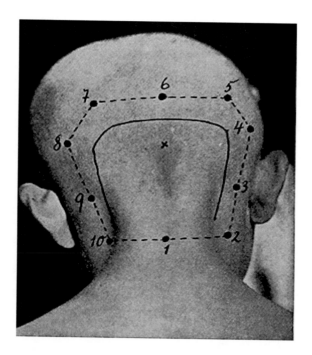

NOTHING A GOOD OLD FASHIONED LOBOTOMY WON'T CURE. HOWEVER, YOU MIGHT WANT TO START WITH THE FRONT INSTEAD OF THE BACK OF THE HEAD.

Of course, this is a more permanent remedy that will unfortunately leave you catatonic once the Hair's reign is over, but what will you care? Your brain's now a vegetable.

On the upside, you will probably now be able to blend in better.

For Those on Staff

You will have to compliment the Naval Narcissist at every chance you can get. Current staffers rate mentioning his name and agreeing with him or flattery every 5 seconds. You can repeat yourself as much as you want, he won't notice.

Take notes, lots of notes. Keep journals of notes. Vats of journals full of notes. Learn from Comey, write everything down.

Whenever the Orange Anus gets you in a room, especially if he gets you in a room alone – write down everything he says afterwards (if you can tape the meetings, even better. Just set your iPhone to record, he'll never notice because he doesn't even know iPhones can do anything other than send Tweets or take calls).

After your meetings, make sure to leak those notes to whomever you can as back-up.

Put a set in a vault somewhere too and bury another set under the ground – we hear the White House rose garden has excellent soil for such a thing.

For the Feminist

Protesting, letter writing, displays of anger, disgust and solidarity – for sure...

But also, vodka, lots of vodka (This book is about survival after all. Do you really think that's possible without alcohol?)

For the Fashionista

Your world is silk and sweaters, shoes and chiffon. No need to interrupt your spending spree. Burry yourself in yards or organza and shop your cares away. Go buy out every crazy trend you want. Indulge yourself like there's no tomorrow, because, you know there may not be. If we're all going to hell in a handbasket – you might as well be well dressed for the occasion.

For the Passive Aggressivist

Dress your cat up in cute, little outfits and share the photos on Instagram.

Then take the cat piss soaked outfits, put them in a large envelope festooned with "Make America Great Again" stickers and anonymously send these to the White House care of The Commander in Chief.

Note: you can also do this with a baby and send the outfits with piles of poop back to him – however, the postage will be slightly more expensive.

For the Optimist

Get knocked up (as long as you're going to be nauseous and binge eating Ben 'n Jerry's anyway, you might as well have a good excuse).

Maybe you can home grow the next President. Maybe there will still be a world left that isn't destroyed by climate change, nuclear attack, economic crisis or civil unrest for that child to grow up in.

Maybe your child won't be fat, or gay, or a girl, or many of the myriad different groups that Trumpalooza is targeting for extinction.

THAT'S RIGHT, SUZY SUNSHINE, FOR YOU,
THE GLASS IS ALWAYS HALF FULL.

For The Aviator

Save up to buy yourself a small plane so that you can make a quick getaway in case of accidental nuclear code launching.

Or stick around, discover a more patriotic, less self-serving approach and take up skywriting. A few choice words written up where thousands can see them at a time can linger a lot longer than a couple of temporary Tweets.

How about doing some sky high rabble rousing and incite the masses to rebel? Or at least zap a few zingers up, up, up in the air where it'll give SCROTUS an itch in a place he can't scratch.

For the Artist

Set aside sunnier subjects and tell it like it is.

Use your art as a form of resistance.

Make a statement, whether it be through painting or poetry; photography or mime (though portraying Yam Head with his mouth shut will definitely be more of a challenge).

Keep in mind, nothing will piss Dolt 45 off more than mocking him. Photoshop away!

For the Alec Baldwin Fans

Revel in the fact that at least Alec will have a steady gig for as long as he wants it on SNL.

For the Staff of SNL

Two words – job security.

For the Traveler

Move to Canada.

If you speak French and don't mind freezing your baguettes off, consider Montreal. Better yet, head to France, where they actually like their President. After all, we've been personally invited by President Macron, who posted a speech on Twitter offering up France as our second homeland. The lines there are probably shorter to get a passport at anyway.

If you don't speak French or are lactose intolerant, but feel confident in your two years of high school Spanish, consider Mexico, where at least there will be a wall to protect you from the shit going on in the U.S.

For the Masochist

Have all of your teeth extracted one day at a time sans Novocaine. The physical pain will outweigh emotional scarring. When you're done with your teeth, consider taking up mixed martial arts at an underground fight club where everyone is bigger and hairier than you are.

Or strap tiny electrodes to your private parts and hand the switch over to someone who really hates you, telling them to have at it.

Or smear anchovy paste all over your body and go for a swim at a piranha park.

Or give yourself a million paper cuts and dive into a shark tank.

For the Broke Masochist

Move back in with your parents.

What with your mom coming up with new chores for you to do, and having to listen to your folks bickering and enduring your dad's snoring and the cat peeing on all of your clothes and the elderly dogs without bladder control, that need to be walked every two seconds – you'll be too exhausted, deaf and sleep deprived to care about anything else that's going on in the world.

For the Passive Aggressivist Who Likes to Cook

Enter a chili cook-off in every electoral state that voted for Trump and cook a delicious, addictive batch laced with laxatives – then lock yourself in the one Port-a-Potty available.

THAT'S NASTY!

For the Undeclared College Student

Student loans racking up and you're wondering just how you'll fit into Trumpalooma's America once you get out of school? Consider changing your major not to Joan, but to Freud. Psychology is the new hip, happening major. The need for shrinks is at an all-time high, thanks to El Cheetohead making America insecure again.

America's psyche, even after the Orange Anus has left the building, will not be totally repaired. Who knows what the lasting effects on innocent people will be to having a pompous, impulse-challenged infant with a narcissistic personality disorder in charge of our nation.

We're talking a huge client base that's going to need your help for years and years to recover.

That means those student loans will be paid off in no-time.

True, our health care system will be in the toilet by the time you get out – but don't worry, there will be plenty of folks willing to forgo food and shelter so they can pay for their daily and weekly sessions with you.

Plus, you'll have something to barter with if say you need a heart transplant or your skin falls off from flesh eating bacteria that will enter through an infected hangnail when you take that water skiing vacation in polluted waters from all that pipeline action.

For the Revisionist

Live your life in denial. Life is what you make it. By that thinking, live your life as if Hillary won. Keep yourself in an isolation tank or locked in your home and shut off any input from the external world – then reimagine everything. Undo years of damage caused by Hair Gropenfuhrer.

For the Party Planner

Start working on your ultimate end of days celebration (given how the Pumpkin Fuhrer is conducting himself with foreign nations and ignoring climate change, it might be here sooner than you think.)

Make elaborate paper-machete Trump-head piñatas and fill them with coal. You may substitute coal for cow dung if you're not offended by the smell – also makes a great garden fertilizer.

POOP AND PINATAS, A MATCH MADE IN HEAVEN.

For the Overly Prepared Optimist

Imagine Michelle Obama decides to run for President in a few years. Start making signs.

For the Protestors

Take that zeal you used to have to follow "The Grateful Dead" to every arena and channel it by enlisting in the Pussy Protest Brigade. Join every march, protest and activist group against Trumplstiltski that you can find.

Fill your Twitter and Facebook feeds with Anti-Trump support groups and stay vigilant for any new activity that might require your voice.

Make witty signs, banners and t-shirts sending the message that we're not going to take it anymore.

Go around collecting signatures on the latest letters and messages to send to congress. Start a letter writing campaign to make positive change.

Devote your life to finding a way to impeach Bratman.

For the Vindictive

Fill the Hair's Twitter account with *tips* that list thousands of high school students from across the country that have been planted as sleeper cells, who will show up at random press events throughout the next four years to ask questions that are intended just to make him look bad.

For the Lapsed 12 Steppers

Join a Surviving Trump support group. Share horror stories while consuming copious amounts of booze and drugs. Sure you're fucking up your life, but now you can at least toss the blame onto Cheeto Benito and get away with it.

Besides, what's the point of getting through it one day at a time if the world will probably not be here when it's over.

For the Theatrical

Spin your sass and lob sarcasms at Strumpf's sophistry. The theatre used to be used to fight injustice and zap zingers in the guise of a song. Look at Broadways' past – *The Sound of Music's* *"Adelweiss"* was sung so the Von Traps could escape the Nazis in a bit of singing subterfuge; and check out the not-so-subtle subtext of every tune in *Cabaret*.

Shakespeare knew the way to rouse the groundlings to action with murder and mayhem (and plenty of snarky humor).

Musicals send their message in-tune and a song being sung by Audrey McDonald or Patti Lupone, Nathan Lane or Lin Manuel Miranda may sound just as sweet (okay, so maybe we're not fabulous with the Shakespeare analogies— you can't say we didn't try).

But Broadway babies need to step up their game and get into the action. Maybe make *Avenue Q, Part Two* and write a song about Cheetolini. Where are those angsty puppets when you need them?

The cast of Hamilton knew how to shine a spotlight on the Babyhands administration. Talk about not throwing away your shot – they made the most of the moment when Pence stepped into the room where it happens.

Remember how Drumpfus was Tweeting about it for weeks? You know he must've eaten his way through every Dunkin' Doughnuts in town after that.

If all else fails, we can always sick Barbra Streisand on him.

For the Pious

Pray that the Barbecued Brutus gets ousted soon or has a change of heart and decides to go back to playing with his own toys instead of our beleaguered nation. If the Pope can endure shaking Orangina's hand and get his photo taken next to that smarmy, smiling Alfred E. Neuman clone, then maybe there's hope for us all.

For the Proactive

Start campaigning for the next Presidential election. It's never too soon to make change.

If you have a problem with the person running against Trumpy Cat, get it out of your system now and deal with it so that you're free as a bird and ready to overthrow Cinnamon Hitler when the time comes.

For the Litigious Proactive

Can you say impeach? Make it so.

For the Athlete

Train for a sport as if you were going to the Olympics. Olympic athletes train all day and night, taking a break only for sleeping and eating. If you're that focused on something else you won't have time to watch the news or look at Facebook long enough to discover our world is going down the toilet. Besides, you might just become our next big hope for shot-putter or win the gold in billiards (our next Olympic sport).

Spend all of your time and efforts tuning out all media in order to focus on becoming the next world ping pong champion; or practice your game of darts using little big hands as your target.

For the Madonna Fan

When Trump says that he doesn't need daily security briefings because he is "like a smart person," imaging him singing it to the tune of Madonna's *Like a Virgin*.

"

"Like a smart person, thinking for the very first time. Like a sm-a-a-a-rt person. Feel your brainwaves next to mine."

For the Fitness Fanatic

Take your angst out on your abs. We're talking crunches, lunges, squats, sphincter-popping pelvic squeezes that will make you sweat, tingle and puke – that's how fabulous they are. When you're done with those, jog it out. Then walk. Then run full throttle as if your life depended on it. Pretend you are the Gingerbread Man and Trump is the wicked witch who wants to catch you, crisp you up and turn you into a giant s'more.

Then add some weights. Being able to lift large weights will come in handy if, say, you need to store gallons of water in an underground bunker before the bombs hit home. Think of how popular your strength and speed will be in situations of life or death.

The Hunger Games could be a cautionary tale in Trumplestiltskin's America. And that extra pudge that most of us carry around could end up making us a menu item rather than an asset, if we end up in an apocalyptic no-food situation (remember that movie *Alive* about the Uruguayan rugby team stranded in the Andes?)

For the Chef with a Sweet Tooth

If baking puts your mind at ease, by all means, go full-out babka for as long as you need to. Bake cookies, cakes, breads, pastries, pies – sweet and savory. Package your goods and sell them, donating all proceeds to the ACLU, so they can fight the damage being caused by Little Lady Fingers.

For the Survivalist

Spend the next four years living in the mountains. Go full Robinson Caruso and create your own sustainable living space. Stock up on water, SPAM and weaponry. If glamping is you're your speed, grab an air mattress, a generator, synthetic fur and a survivalist sous chef with a hot bod for company, so you don't get hungry or lonely and start drawing faces on volleyballs.

For Those with the Munchies

Kick back and munch on Nachos, Doritos and Cheetos (kick it up a notch with the fiery hot Cheetos to "feel the burn.")

For the Nature Lover

Take a hike – consider hitting the trails for a

few years. Seek out the wide opened country and mountain regions with sparse population to avoid hearing any bad news. An added plus is you might just survive if the country is plunged into a full-scale war. Plus, you always wanted to learn the banjo.

If you're more of a sun person, check out the desert, where you can literally bury your head in the sand. Pitch a tent at Burning Man and take up residence there. Just invest in plenty of sun block and bottled water.

For the Sports Spectator

Get wrapped up in football season and go to as many NFL games as you can or watch them on TV, DVR'd if necessary. Run your football fantasy leagues too.

Then, before you know it, Basketball season will be here. Go to those NBA games. Mix in some hockey and support the NHL.

Of course. you can't miss America's favorite pastime. Baseball season will keep you busy busy busy. Go to those home games every night if need be. Your team needs you.

While you're at it, mix in some NASCAR racing and don't forget your tennis whites for all those cups and opens.

And then there's golf, the PGA can certainly take up your time even if it is as exciting as watching paint dry sometimes. What do you care, it'll keep your mind on the game and off Hair Furor.

For the Scientific

If you're a rocket scientist, you're in luck.

All those years training to be an astro-physicist have prepared you to find a way off this planet; which will probably be a good thing considering once Trumplestiltskin cuts all the funding to stop global warming, and given the odds that he flips his wig and mishandles the nuclear football because one more *Saturday Night Live* skit puts him over the edge, you will be lucky to be able to sustain life on another planet – preferably not an orange one.

GET READY TO GET OUT OF DODGE.

For the Horror Fan

Find out who recited the chant unleashing unending evil from "The Evil Dead" and get him to put Cheeto Benito back into his box. See if Bruce Campbell is available and make sure to watch out for pussy-grabbing trees. While you're at it toss in some of those Ray Harryhausen skeletons, maybe they can help.

THIS NEW DIET HAS ME LOOKING JUST LIKE JOHNNY DEPP.

For the Satirist

Write your own goddamned book. I'm doing my part.

6

STICKS AND STONES

How many nicknames can you think of to call The Hair?

Here's a few we can think of to get you started:

Dolt.45

El Cheetohead

PeeOTUS

Sir Babyhands

The Hair

Orangina

Flaming Cheetohead

Drumpfus

Cheeto-in-Chief

Fuckface-von-clownstick

The Combover Con Artist

Cheeto Benito

Trumplestiltskin

Donald Chump

Benedict Donald

The Tweeting Tyrant

The Angry Creamsicle

Adolf Twitler

Agent Orange

Hair Fuhrer

Prima Donald

Mango Mussolini

King Leer

Naval Narcissist

Pumpkin Spice Satan

Tangerine Nutsack

Tang Tyrant

Putin's Putty

Fanta Fascist

The Angry Yam

Nacho Nazi

Orange Anus

Don the Con

Cheeto Satan

Fake President

Trumpty Dumpty

Sir Sissypants

The Angry Creamsicle

Darth Hater

Dorbel

SCROTUS

Putin's Puppet

Hair Hitler

Trump of Doom

Man Baby

Dotard

Fopdoodle

For more Nasty Woman's Guides, including **The Nasty Woman's Guide to Surviving Trump Coloring and Activity Book,** and to join our email list, check out our website at:

www.nastywomansguide.com

ABOUT THE AUTHOR

Nas T. Girl has been writing humor professionally for a very long time, and has been unprofessional even longer.

She has a B.A. in English from The University of California, Berkeley, which qualifies her to basically be broke and liberal for the rest of her life; and has been honing her nasty girl skills ever since being a nice girl got her nowhere.

She tried to knit herself a pink pussy hat but kept making knots instead of knits.

She's done her fair share of marching against injustice and no, she did not vote for Fuckface von Clownstick.

63256147R10042

Made in the USA
San Bernardino, CA
19 December 2017